Contents

What Your Horse Needs — 4

Emotional Systems — 12

Learning Theory — 19

Learning Positive, Negative, & Combined Reinforcement — 25

The Importance of Timing — 32

Reinforcement History — 38

Threshold — 44

Choice — 51

Contents

How Horses See — 58

Breath Communication — 64

Opposition Reflex — 70

Interpretation of Body Language — 77

Habituation — 84

Learned Helplessness — 90

Scientific Method — 95

What Horses Need

01
What Horses Need

The three F's: Freedom, Forage and Friends.

Freedom to move and express natural behaviours – which studies show are not available to them in a stall.
Forage to satisfy their evolutionary need to graze 18 hours per day and keep their digestive tract healthy.
Friends to interact with and help them be mentally stimulated and feel safe.

While we aren't always able to keep our horses in as natural an environment as we'd like, with full access to the three F's, we can do our best to keep these three basic needs in mind. My old horses are stalled in bad weather, but they get time out of their stall every day to roll and stretch their legs, and their other two F's are well covered.

Many horses aren't able to eat for 18 hours a day, but as long as their diet is mostly forage based, they eat as much of their day as we can manage, and they have Freedom and Friends, they should do well. Some horses may not be able to live in a herd, but with lots of Forage and Freedom, as well as equine interaction across a fence, or reliable interactions with humans or other animals, many horses can do well.

What Horses Need

The best is, of course, if they are able to have sufficient access to all three. Studies have even shown that horses who live in a herd in a more natural environment are able to focus on learning new skills more easily, and pick up new lessons more quickly than horses who don't have the opportunity to live in a herd on pasture. Also, be aware of your feeding schedule if your horse isn't on free choice forage – try to time your training sessions for when they have a full tummy; no one can learn on an empty stomach, and your horse is no exception.

If you are having an issue with your horse, first check that it is not a physical issue. That means confirming that you've done all you can to give them a horse friendly living situation, and ruling out any physical pain from lameness, body pain or dental issues. Working with a horse is truly a collaboration, and you will want to have a good relationship with not only your horse, but your veterinarian, farrier and bodyworker as well.

What Horses Need

REMEMBER: The three F's of a happy horse: Freedom, Forage and Friends

My Experience

What Horses Need

It was January 2019. There was a ton of snow, and frigid cold, and my dad was in the hospital, recently diagnosed with stage four cancer. One morning, during chores, I noticed Oly was lame.

I wasn't sure which leg he was lame on – he seemed sort of all over sore, but I watched him and he seemed to get around okay, I watched him drink and eat, and decided to wait until the next day when my farrier was coming and get his thoughts. Any other time, I probably would've made him a vet appointment, but he didn't seem in any urgent distress and I didn't have the bandwidth to deal with another issue that day.

The farrier and I went over him the next day, and decided he was mostly lame on his left front, but he was quite sore in his withers and off-ish on his other front and a hind leg too. Our best hypothesis was that he'd fallen on the ice and was generally body sore.

I chatted with my vet, and they suggested some anti-inflammatories for a few days along with small pen rest so he was moving but not too much, and if he didn't improve they should see him.

My dad's health continued to deteriorate and he passed away within the month from when Oly first looked sore.

After his funeral, Oly was still lame, though much more solidly on his left front, so the vet came out to see him. After a physical exam, they felt we were right in our initial thought of a soft tissue injury, and since he hadn't improved on pen rest, we moved him to a stall. They said it might take time, months, to heal, so we planned on keeping him in long term.

Oly hated the stall. We had kids camps running that summer and fall, and had to park carts in front of Oly's stall to keep people away from him, as he was all pinned ears and teeth for anyone but me.

We did our best to keep him as comfortable as possible. We kept him on anti-inflammatories in case he was painful, but that made no difference in his lameness, so likely his behaviour wasn't pain related. We kept hay in front of him constantly. We made sure he got a short turnout daily, prioritizing his mental health over any potential setbacks. We kept another horse in the barn with him all the time. We had a bodyworker do massage treatments on him.

Winter arrived again, but Oly hadn't improved, and by then he'd been in small pen or stall rest for getting close to a year. We decided to x-ray, and found that he had advanced arthritis in his shoulder, evidently a result of blunt force trauma. At this point, we thought we'd start turning him out and see how it affected his lameness, but he promptly developed a nasty skin condition that required clipping, and since it was in the middle of a Canadian winter, that meant even more stalling for Oly.

Beyond his aggression with humans in his barn, Oly – always a timid fellow – became hyper spooky. Getting a blanket on and off (a necessity given his skin issues!) was a huge ordeal. I had to tape up any straps before I even tried, as one dangling would send him crashing into stall walls, or into me. He was dangerous he was so afraid, and everyday handling was an ordeal.

When he was finally able to go back to living outdoors with the herd, he'd been in a small pen or stall for 18 months. While he wasn't sound, he also didn't get more sore outside, and we quickly transitioned him back into the main herd, where he lives very happily to this day.

"Happily" is the key here – once he was back living outdoors with his friends, he was like a different horse. Instead of being cranky with people, he would walk up and ask sweetly for a treat. Instead of spooking at everything, he would explore new things with curiosity. Even now, though, he still doesn't like to come into the barn, even for just his routine hoof care. You can tell he is worried that we'll make him stay again.

What Horses Need

It really got me thinking how many horses who live in a stall most of their lives have behavioural challenges that would be resolved simply by changing their living situation. We had to try stall rest, to give Oly the best chance to heal his injury – but so many horses who live in stalls are there for owner convenience or because of some human need to keep them from getting a scratch or a sunburnt mane before the big show. I wonder how much better their performance would be at the show, however, if they had the opportunity to live like a horse.

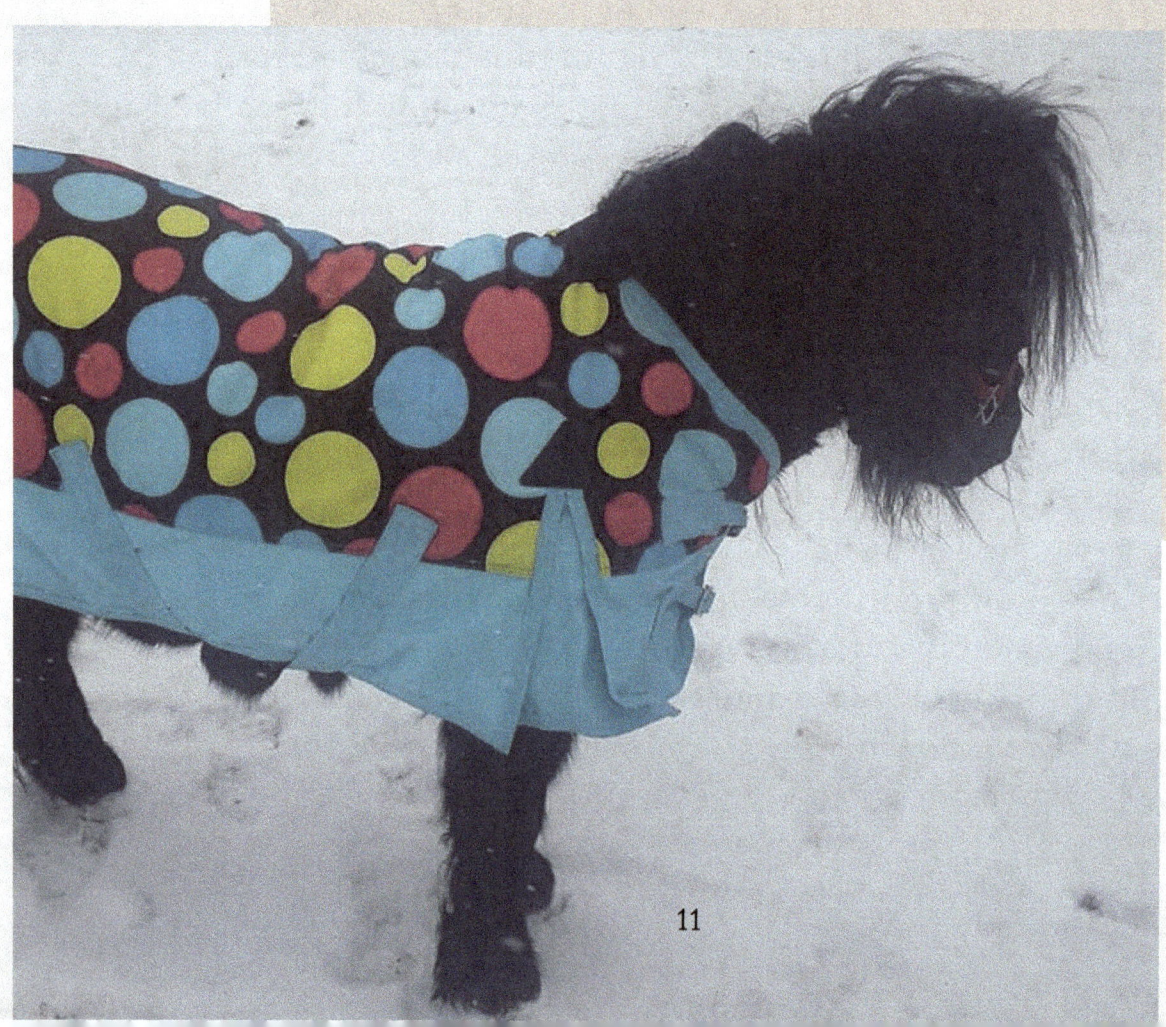

Emotional Systems 02

Jaak Panksepp, affective neuroscience researcher, has identified seven emotional systems that are at the core of all emotions in all animals (humans too!) Understanding these seven systems really helps us keep our horse's emotions in mind during our training. (If you'd like to learn more about Dr. Panksepp's research, I suggest starting with his TED talk.)

Emotional Systems

SEEKING – SEEKING is the problem-solving aspect of a horse's brain. In the wild, this system would keep them learning about their environment, finding food, water, companionship and safety. This is an important emotional system for training, as it's this one we want to engage most often. A horse who is curious and engaged in learning is operating within the SEEKING system.

CARE – Building relationships is an important aspect of the life of a herd animal. We need to be sure we're taking time to engage the CARE system, rather than simply drilling skills. Spending time just being with our horse, finding their favourite scratching spots, and connecting with them through the CARE system is an important aspect of building a connection. The CARE system can also be an important tool to bring a horse back out of the FEAR, RAGE, or PANIC systems.

PLAY – The PLAY system is engaged when horses are feeling comfortable with their herdmates. If you don't see your horse engaging their PLAY then it is a good sign they are feeling stressed in general. Incorporating PLAY into your time with your horse is another way to build your bond and relationship.

LUST – The LUST system is a biological imperative, and something to keep in mind during our training of stallions especially, but mares as well, and to a lesser extent, geldings. Punishing behaviour that is a result of the engagement of the LUST system is rarely effective, and it is much better to redirect and try to re-engage their SEEKING system instead.

FEAR – The FEAR system evolved to keep the horse safe from danger. When the FEAR system is engaged, it activates the horse's parasympathetic nervous system: the flight or fight response. Their heart rate and respiratory rate increase, and other biological changes take place, preparing them to run away from danger, or if they are unable to run, to fight. Unfortunately, horses displaying behaviour as a result of the FEAR system are often punished, when what they need is reassurance and engagement of the CARE or SEEKING systems.

RAGE – RAGE is very often the result of a prolonged FEAR response, or continued presence of other stressors. CARE is a good way to combat RAGE, but ideally, we avoid getting them into that system at all.

PANIC/GRIEF – Most often seen during forced separation from herdmates, PANIC/GRIEF is very closely related to the FEAR system. Called names like "herdbound", this behaviour is often dismissed or punished. Seen commonly during abrupt weaning, or when a special friend is separated, this is a very strong emotional system in the horse, due to their reliance on their herdmates for safety and security.

Emotional Systems

Emotional Systems

REMEMBER:

Understanding and recognizing the emotional systems of your horse will help you maintain their ability to learn and keep a good association with training. Most importantly, learn to engage the SEEKING system, and recognize and avoid the FEAR system.

My Experience

Emotional Systems

I've handled stallions a lot, for as long as I can remember.

When I went to college and during my early years at the vet clinic, I handled stallions of every size, Quarter Horses, Arabians, Warmbloods, Percherons, and even a bucking horse.

Stallions tend to be difficult, not because they're mean, but because they're easily distracted and it can be very hard to get them to keep their attention on you. And when their attention isn't on you, then they can easily run over you or drag you off without noticing.

Before I understood the emotional systems and how positive reinforcement works in the horse's brain, I was trying to handle stallions by "being the boss mare" and trying to keep their attention through brute force. That meant a lot of yelling (because of their familiarity with an angry mare, stallions tend to notice yelling more than force) and jerking on the lead (with a chain when we're talking about the full sized horses) and making them back up to try and re-engage their thinking brain and distract them from "stallion thoughts".

Emotional Systems

It wasn't that it didn't work, but it was risky, required physical strength, and wasn't much fun for anyone involved.

Frankie was a yearling when I really started focusing on exploring positive reinforcement and the science that backs it up. One of the first things I did was going out and teaching Frankie and his brother Johnnie to touch a target, which of course they took to in no time.

For Frankie especially, who was a reactive and suspicious youngster, the target became a great tool for teaching him new things and helping him build his confidence, so by the time he was maturing as a stallion, the target was a very solidly understood skill.

When Frankie would go all "stallion" on me, screaming at the mares and trying to drag me towards them, instead of thinking that he was "bad" and I needed to get after him, I had more understanding that it was simply a biological function of his LUST system, and instead of fighting it, I needed to redirect him.

That was as simple as offering him a target. By saying, "Frankie, can you touch?" and holding out the back of my hand I was able to nearly instantly turn down the LUST system and turn on the SEEKING system. He would nicker and touch my hand, earn a treat (or sometimes just praise if I didn't happen to have one), and then continue walking along beside me on a loose lead, focused on me instead of the mares until a new distraction presented itself, in which case the target would be there to help me again.

Really being aware that your horse's emotions are not always in their control can make us much more empathetic trainers. They can't control that they're afraid, their FEAR system is there to protect them. They can't control that they're in the PANIC/GRIEF system because they're by themselves … but we can.

While research into equine emotions is still ongoing and not yet entirely understood, just keeping their emotions in mind when trying to figure out how to deal with our horse's behaviour is going to help us be much kinder and more effective.

Learning Theory
03

Learning theory is a scientific principle of how learning takes place. Learning is a result of either reinforcing a desired behaviour or punishing an undesired behaviour.

Both reinforcement and punishment can be positive or negative. In this context, positive and negative don't mean good and bad, but instead think of them mathematically: positive means adding something, and negative means taking something away.

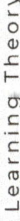
Learning Theory

Positive Reinforcement, then, means you're adding something the horse finds valuable as a reward for getting the response you were looking for.

Negative reinforcement includes traditional pressure and release techniques, with an aversive stimulus being removed as a result of the correct behaviour being demonstrated.

Positive punishment involves the addition of an aversive, following an undesired behaviour, and negative punishment would be the withholding of something good, until the poor behaviour stops.

All training approaches and techniques can be explained using learning theory. When we learn a new technique, it's important to understand where it fits on this chart, so we are able to use the technique effectively, and possibly even decide if it's something we're comfortable applying to our own horses.

While both positive reinforcement and negative reinforcement can, if used appropriately, be very effective training methods, they do result in very different emotional responses from the horse (more on that next chapter.) Timing is very important in either method, but poor timing in positive reinforcement simply means the horse won't learn as quickly, or might learn the wrong thing. Poor timing in negative reinforcement can result in quickly becoming positive punishment, as well as creating a very fearful and confused horse.

Learning Theory

REMEMBER: All learning happens through reinforcement or punishment. Both can be either positive (adding something) or negative (taking something away) – which does not mean good or bad.

My Experience

Learning Theory

I was standing in a circle of friends and family at a horse show, just chatting as we often do.

I don't remember how it came up or what the context was, but someone said, "Kendra's horses know better than to step out of line." They meant it as a compliment, I think, and everyone else standing there laughed and agreed, but it was the first time that I thought, "Wait, is that what I want?"

I didn't want my horse to do what I wanted because they were afraid of the consequences if they didn't. But I also didn't know any other way.

I remember telling people, "oh, I feed my horses treats, but never during training" because I thought that was right. I didn't think treats were "real training", which is why my first inadvertent attempts at using positive reinforcement was teaching Hawk tricks, as a last ditch effort to build a relationship with him.

That's the case with so many of us – changing the way you've always done something is hard, so it takes a very challenging horse to shake us out of the status quo and open our minds to new ideas.

I was willing to use food rewards in trick training, because it wasn't "real" training, just silly tricks.

Of course, I was wrong about that too, because horses don't know the difference between "serious training" and "silly trick training" – it's all just learning to them.
But when I started teaching Hawk tricks, things changed.

Like I'd hoped, our relationship improved. He was more engaged, not just when we were working on trick training and food was involved, but in everything we did together. I remember saying, "I know it's crazy, but I swear teaching him tricks made him smarter!"

It wasn't crazy.

He was more engaged, because I was finally communicating in a way he understood. Instead of pressuring him into the right answer, I was letting him use his innate problem-solving skills, looking for the signs he was on the right track, and giving him a food reward to make it super clear that he was right.

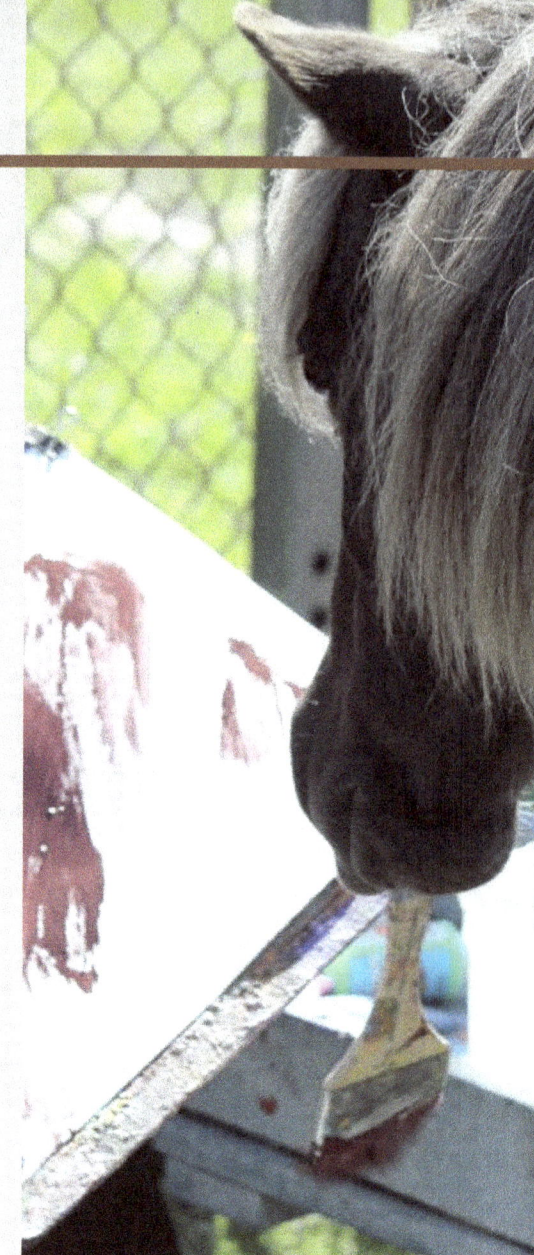

Learning Theory

It seemed like he was smarter because problem solving actually builds new pathways in his brain – he WAS getting smarter!

He'd learned how to learn.

It was years later before I finally figured out that this sort of training wasn't just for silly tricks, but was equally effective in training absolutely everything, with all the added benefits I saw in my relationship with Hawk thrown in for good measure!

Using Positive, Negative & Combined Reinforcement

Positive reinforcement, or reward-based training, uses the horse's SEEKING system to help guide them to the right answer, then rewards with something that the horse values.

Food is a primary reinforcer, as it's something the horse needs to survive and therefore values very highly. As such, food is a very powerful tool, but praise, scratches and rest can all be used as positive reinforcement as well. The important thing is that it's something the horse values, and what they value most will vary depending on the individual.

For positive reinforcement to be clearly understood by your horse, a marker or bridge signal is used to mark the moment that they gave the correct response, to bridge the gap until you are able to give the reward. A bridge signal could be a clicker, or any other sound or signal, as long as you are consistent.

Contrary to popular belief, horses do not become mouthy when food rewards are used. They become mouthy when they believe that is what earns them a reward. When they are taught how to be calm around food, and that their behaviour is what results in a food reward, training with the use of food actually results in less mouthy and rude behaviour, as that is no longer rewarding for them.

Negative reinforcement is traditional pressure and release training. An aversive stimulus is applied (pressure, tap, etc) and removed when the correct response is given. An aversive could be as soft as the pressure of squaring your shoulders and stepping towards your horse, or it could be a tap of a stick or whip.

Reinforcement

It's important to avoid increasing the aversive stimulus when using negative reinforcement, as if you don't get a response, it's likely that your horse doesn't understand, and you need to change and take a slightly different approach instead. Timing is also very important; the aversive is removed the second the correct response is given. In early training, even an effort or a small step in the right direction must be marked by removal of the pressure, or your horse will get discouraged, or even fearful.

In positive reinforcement, the SEEKING system is engaged, and the horse has a very good association with things learned using this method. Eventually, the behaviour itself will take on the same emotional association as the food reward, and in some cases the behaviour will be self rewarding. Horses can sometimes become frustrated trying to find the right answer, but targets and other tools can help to guide them.

Negative reinforcement, if done gently and with careful timing, is also effective, but is unlikely to have as positive an emotional response from the horse. If the timing is poor, it is easy to push them into the FEAR system, so care must be taken to read their responses and adjust accordingly.

Combined reinforcement is the term for the use of both positive and negative reinforcement to teach a behaviour (skill). Negative reinforcement is used to help guide the horse towards the right answer, and when they give a response that is on the right track, the pressure is removed AND is coupled with a positive reinforcement reward. This can be a very powerful tool as well, but care must be taken to use the least invasive, minimally aversive form of negative reinforcement possible to avoid creating a poor association with your positive reinforcement.

Using Reinforcement

REMEMBER: Positive reinforcement involves the use of a marker or bridge signal to mark the moment the desired response is given, followed by a reward. Negative reinforcement uses the removal of an aversive stimulus to mark the correct response. Combined reinforcement uses both the removal of an aversive stimulus AND the addition of a reward.

My Experience

Using Positive, Negative & Combined Reinforcement

When I first heard about teaching a horse to touch a target I thought, okay, I'm sure I can teach them to touch a target … but why? What good would it do to have a horse touch something with their nose on cue?

Then I watched a video from Connection Training, where they were using a target to teach a horse to load happily into a trailer, and I thought, aha, there's the reason I was looking for!

But I was still skeptical that it was going to be as effective as they described. I decided that the only way to really learn about it and decide it's value was to try it myself.

I had a little rainbow crop that I'd bought only because of how cute it was, and I drafted it as a target, armed myself with a pocket full of cookies, and went out to the pen that housed my two yearlings – Frankie and Johnnie.

Reinforcement

It took no more than five minutes to teach them that touching the end of the crop earned a cookie, and we all had fun.

But that wasn't the test — I'd already been sure I could teach them to touch a target, the test came the next day!

I spread out a tarp, which neither baby had ever seen before and tried to walk them over it. First up was Johnnie.

Johnnie walked happily up to the tarp, stopped dead and put on that patented "NO" face they have, nose wrinkled, ears back, expression clear that he was NOT going to step on that weird thing.

Until I showed him the target.

I swear his ears came up so fast you could almost hear a "ding" sound.

"Oh, this is a fun target game!" he thought, and happily stepped onto the tarp to touch his target and earn a treat. I turned him around and headed for the tarp again and he stomped over cheerfully.

Frankie was next and while Johnnie was a confident and bold youngster, Frankie was not – everything was scary for him and he was very cautious about anything new.

I couldn't even get him to walk close to the tarp, he stopped several feet away and blew at it.

When I showed him his target, it wasn't quite as immediate as it was for confident Johnnie, but with just four touches of the target Frankie was across the tarp as well, and happy to walk over it again a second time.

To this day, both those colts (now coming eight year old geldings) have a very positive association with a tarp, to the point that Johnnie will wander off during a liberty training session just to walk over the tarp.

I don't think there's any way that I would've been able to teach them to walk over a tarp that quickly with that sort of positive experience using my previous knowledge and methods.
The power of having them move towards something they value (a target and resulting food reward), instead of away from something aversive (halter pressure) was made so clear to me. While I already believed in the power of positive reinforcement in general, this experiment with target training is what made me shift away from relying on traditional pressure and release methods.

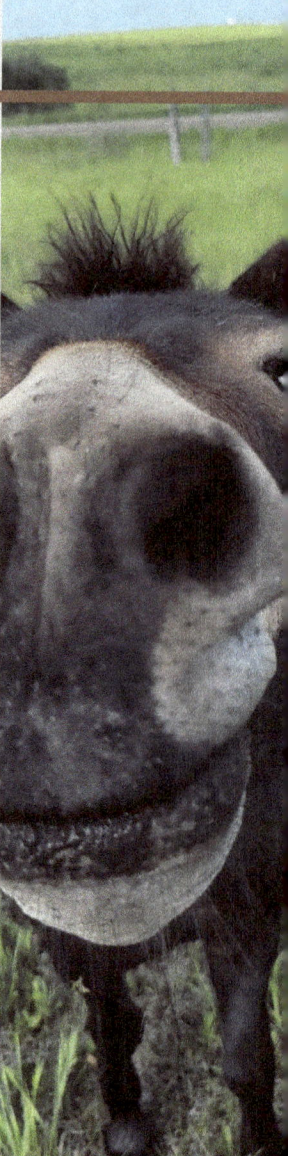

The Importance of Timing

Regardless of which form of reinforcement you're using (positive or negative, or combined) the better your timing is, the more effective the training will be.

For positive reinforcement, that means that timing of your marker signal – I use the word "good," but you could use a click or whistle, and I've even heard of people using a touch or a hand signal for a deaf horse. You want to be sure to mark the moment that your horse begins to give you the right answer, so they know that was the decision that earned them the reward. The marker signal will become very valuable, and an excellent form of communication to clarify exactly what behaviour you liked and want to see more of.

The good news about positive reinforcement is that if your timing is bad, the worst thing that might happen is you accidentally reinforce the wrong thing, and you have to go back and try again to fix it. No harm, no foul, and no hard feelings on the part of your horse.

For negative reinforcement, timing is everything. It's the difference between clearly explaining to your horse what you're looking for, and punishing them for a reason they don't understand. It's critical to remove the pressure as soon as you get any response from the horse in the early stages of learning, or they'll get discouraged and either try another response you don't like as much, be pushed into FEAR or even RAGE, or simply shut down entirely and not give any response.

Remember, the horse doesn't know what you want until you give them a chance to learn it. Regardless of which form of reinforcement you're using, you must reinforce every tiny effort along the way, to show them they are on the right track. If you try to wait to reinforce the completed skill or behaviour, you'll have a frustrated/fearful/shut down horse and won't be any closer to getting the response you wanted.

That means we need to reward the "try", sometimes even if it isn't the right answer, and then continue to build the small efforts until we get the finished response we are looking for.

Go slow, you'll get there faster.

Timing

The Importance of Timing

REMEMBER: Regardless of the training technique you use, the accuracy of your timing will have a direct effect on how quickly your horse is able to learn. Rewarding the effort, and the small steps along the way will result in your horse having a better understanding of the behaviour and will encourage them to continue to offer the next attempt.

My Experience

The Importance of Timing

Many years ago, when I was 13 years old, my Grandad was taking his eight horse hitch to the AMHA World Show in Fort Worth, Texas.

I was super excited, because I was going to get to show there for the first time!

One of my grandad's leaders was a beautiful, talented gelding named Gretz. Named for The Great One of hockey, Gretz was the greatest lead horse my grandad ever had. He had also been a champion halter horse, and I'd shown him to great success in youth classes as well, though I wasn't showing him anymore at home.

Since the days when I'd shown Gretz in showmanship, the standard had improved and a haunch turn was now required. Gretz didn't know how to do a haunch turn, so leading up to our trip to Texas I set out to teach him.

Of course, I was 13 years old, and he was an experienced middle-aged gelding who was set in his ways, so it didn't go that smoothly.

Timing

Every time I asked him for a haunch turn, you could see him trying to figure out what I wanted, but then just sidepass instead. At the time I interpreted it as "I don't know what you want so I'm going to do this thing I already understand" which was probably partially accurate, and which I found equally frustrating and adorable.

In retrospect, I suspect my timing – or lack thereof - had a lot to do my struggling to get the haunch turn.

If I'd removed the pressure at the first step of his front end, he would've understood much more quickly that I only wanted his front end to move. Instead, I thought, yay progress and kept asking and he thought, oh guess that wasn't what she wanted, let's try moving the back end too, usually that's a thing she likes.

We need to reinforce the tiny steps and approximations towards the end goal, or they'll never know when they're on the right track. Timing is so important to help make our training clear to our horse and set them up to learn with confidence and enthusiasm.

Luckily, our horses, like the great Gretz, are very forgiving of our fumbling, and he did finally figure out what the heck I was trying to teach him. If I'd known then what I know now, it would've been much easier for both of us.

Reinforcement History 06

When your horse has a behaviour that they like to repeat, whether it's one you like or not, it's because they have a good reinforcement history for that behaviour. They've learned, whether on purpose or not, that it's going to have a good outcome for them, so they choose to repeat it.

That means that when it's a behaviour you'd rather see less of, you need to make an alternative more rewarding, and build up the reinforcement history to the new behaviour to the point that they default to the new, desirable behaviour instead.

Example One: My yearling colts were behaving like yearling colts and putting everything – including me in their mouths. This was a behaviour they found reinforcing as they'd get a response from me – not a good response, but at their age, any attention was good attention. Using positive reinforcement, I taught them to touch a target and earn a food reward. The biting disappeared, as their new, more rewarding, behaviour took over, and they were instead looking for the next target to touch or game to play to earn a treat.

Example Two: Every day when I went out to feed, Oly would start banging his gate with his front foot with a deafening CLANG CLANG CLANG. He found it rewarding because it was – he'd bang the gate and I would feed him, not because he banged the gate, but because I was going to anyway. The two events weren't linked in my mind, but they were in his: banging the gate = dinner, and some delightful hollering before I got there so he knew I was paying attention to him. 😉 I needed to make the thing I liked (no banging) more rewarding than the thing he liked (banging). Every time he banged the gate, I'd turn my back to him and stand still, until he stopped banging, then I'd keep walking towards him to feed him. If he banged again, I'd stop and turn away. It didn't take him long to learn that banging made the food delivery stop, while being still and quiet made it hurry along the way he wanted. Within a week, the banging had improved to the point that my sanity was saved.

Understanding your horse's reinforcement history can also help if you have a behaviour you'd like to see more of, and they're reluctant to offer. How can you make it more rewarding for them, and build up the reinforcement history to the point that they enjoy the behaviour as much as you do?

Keep in mind, that horses have a reinforcement history with objects and people as well. If they have a good reinforcement history with you, they'll be happy to be caught and engage in whatever new training or adventure you have for them. But if every time you work with them it's a lot of aversives and nothing they find reinforcing, then their emotional and reinforcement history with the training is going to be associated with you as well. Every experience with your horse is adding to their reinforcement history regarding you. While you aren't going to be able to make every experience a rewarding one – there will be health care or other things that just aren't going to be fun for your horse - you'll want the good experiences to far outweigh the bad, for the sake of your relationship and your future successes.

That means we need to reward the "try", sometimes even if it isn't the right answer, and then continue to build the small efforts until we get the finished response we are looking for.

Go slow, you'll get there faster.

Reinforceent History

Remember: Horses will display the behaviour they've found more rewarding. Make the behaviour you like more rewarding and you'll see more of it. Make sure your horse also has a good reinforcement history with you.

My Experience

Reinforcement History

My grandad used to say that he never knew a horse that was any good that was easy to catch on pasture.

He meant that a horse who realized that the pasture was way more fun than working, and was smart enough to know that not being caught was the way to stay there, was probably a smart and energetic horse in work as well – which is just another way of framing reinforcement history. The pasture is more reinforcing than work, while the same horses would line up at the gate to work when they were in a dry lot. Work was more reinforcing for them than a boring pen without grass.

I experienced a huge change when I started shifting my training to using more and more positive reinforcement – suddenly, "work" became more reinforcing than anything.
It turns out, my horses find the combined appeal of the opportunity to earn food rewards and the challenge of problem-solving new skills and showing off established ones MUCH more reinforcing than eating grass with their friends.

Reinforcement History

Today, my biggest problem when I go out to catch a horse to work with the is the number of volunteers trying to come, too!

It's amazing how quickly you can change your horse's reinforcement history with you. Recently I've had horses on antibiotics, both of whom hated the taste of the pills and had to have the dissolved pills syringed into their mouths twice a day.

Both are usually keen and eager to be caught, but within a couple days of twice daily meds, they became very difficult to catch, no matter how I tried to balance the meds with treats and scratches and walks. Once the antibiotics were finished, both horses quickly returned to enjoying their time with me and being eager to put on their halters.

Threshold 07

Threshold is the term for when a horse transitions into their FEAR system, triggering the autonomic functions associated with the fight or flight or freeze response.

When we are working with our horses, we need to be aware of the small signs that they are approaching threshold, so we can adjust our approach to keep them comfortable. A horse cannot learn when they are in the FEAR system, so even if we did get the response we're looking for, they aren't able to retain it.

You cannot erase a fear memory, only do what is possible to overshadow it, so we want to be very careful not to create any fear memories, or we'll be struggling to overcome that memory forever. Signs of approaching threshold may include raised head, widened eyes, flared nostrils, holding breath or snorting, scooting or dancing, but signs will vary depending on the expressiveness of your horse – you need to be familiar with your horse and always be watching to see how they are responding

If you feel your horse is approaching threshold, you can make adjustments to prevent them from going over threshold.

Step back, take a deep breath, and try scratching their withers or other favourite spots. Scratching and rubbing has been shown to lower a horse's heart rate, and will help activate the CARE system, releasing oxytocin to counteract the FEAR response and allow your horse's sympathetic nervous system to re-engage. A good sign that they are beginning to relax is when they lick and chew – the salivary glands are one of the body functions that shuts down during fight or flight, and when they reactivate, you'll see the licking and chewing response.

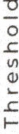
Threshold

Other things can influence threshold besides what you're doing with your horse. Something that usually doesn't bother your horse at all might one day trigger a FEAR reaction. It's called trigger stacking, when a number of things build up so that the horse is nearer to threshold before you ever start, and something that usually is well within their threshold suddenly sends them over. Maybe it's a windy day, or their friend moved to another paddock, or something changed in their environment that you didn't even notice but was a big deal to them.

That's why we need to meet our horse where they are every single day. We must always be aware of the signs they are approaching threshold, so we can make adjustments, both to keep our horse comfortable and able to learn, and to prevent a big, potentially dangerous, fear response.

Threshold

Threshold

REMEMBER: Recognizing the signs that your horse is approaching threshold can help you prevent activation of the FEAR system, during which they cannot learn and will form permanent fear associations with the training. Threshold can change day to day depending on external factors.

My Experience

Threshold

One day, not long after I'd brought Bentley home, I went out to work with him and I couldn't even get close to him.

We'd been making great progress working together at liberty in his pen. He was doing great on his liberty leading, standing, picking up his feet, even giving me the first steps of sidepassing and backing.

On this day, however, I couldn't get within 20 feet of him without him running away.

Once upon a time I would've persevered and insisted that he was going to work today whether he liked it or not. My years of experience in the horse world had ingrained in me the antiquated and ill-advised idea that "you can't let the horse (or mule) win".

Luckily for Bentley, I'd gotten a lot smarter by this point, so instead I just stood and watched him and tried to figure out what had changed? Why was he so nervous all of a sudden?

Threshold

It definitely had to be a conscious choice on my part, as it's hard not to take those moments personally. I was thinking "what did I do wrong?" and "why are you mad at me?"

But once I watched for a bit, and looked around and listened, I realized that the neighbours had weaned their calves, and Bentley was agitated by the cattle bawling and being distressed in the distance.
It wasn't personal at all. He was reacting to something in his environment that had nothing to do with me, or with him.

Since he was already WAY over threshold, trying to do anything with him would've been a bad idea. Instead, I gave him some extra hay to try and distract him and calm him down, and waited until the next afternoon to try again.

The cattle had settled down, and so had Bentley, and he was right back to keen and engaged and ready to play.

I'm so glad I didn't insist that he work with me when he wasn't in a place to handle it, as I'm sure it would've set back our relationship. I'm sure there were times when, if I'd just noticed my horse was having a bad day before we ever started, I could've stopped and taken a day off. It's much better to have no progress than go backwards in your relationship.

08 Choice

Anything you do with your horse is going to be more enjoyable for them, and rewarding for you, if you can allow them to choose to participate.

While it may seem like it isn't possible, in many cases you can give your horse a choice, and reward them when they make the choice that you were looking for. Even just thinking about waiting for them to make the choice can improve your horsemanship and relationship with your horse.

Working with your horse at liberty (with no tack so they have the freedom to walk away) is a hugely valuable tool, both to build the trusting relationship you want with your horse, and to give you more information about how your horse is feeling. I've also found that working at liberty makes me a better trainer, as I have to work to be engaging and rewarding enough to keep the horse interested.

Horses are wired for problem solving – that's the basis of their SEEKING system, allowing them to find the things they needed for survival in the wild. They enjoy problem solving, and if you allow them to find the choice that you are going to reward, they're going to be keen to participate.

Note: for it to be truly a case of choice, even at liberty, if you're training with food rewards, it's important to ensure that they have a full tummy or have access to "free" food, so that they don't feel pressured to respond because of their requirement for food.

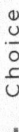

Choice

Incorporating choice in your training is especially valuable when working with a horse who has been bullied or manhandled (intentionally or otherwise – it's far too easy to do with a Miniature Horse) and has a lot of resistance or fear as a result. When you remove the tack, making it clear to the horse that you are not going to force them to participate, it empowers them to engage and learn without worrying that they're not going to be able to walk away. In a very fearful horse, working with them in protective contact (through a fence) may give them even more confidence.

If you want to improve your communication and relationship with your horse, I highly recommend some time spent working at liberty, and doing all you can to listen to your horse's choice in all your handling.

Choice

REMEMBER: Allowing your horse to choose whether or not to participate will make them more engaged, willing learners. Giving them control over their actions will make them feel safer and improve your partnership with your horse.

My Experience

Choice

Once Bentley was comfortable with leading and basic handling in his own pen, and around the barn yard, I wanted to bring him in to the barn.

As always with Bentley, new things are challenging, and I'd set my expectations carefully to be prepared if it didn't work out the first time.

I did have him on a halter and lead, because it wasn't that long after the great mule hunt (when he and his brother escaped from their pen and were lost in the woods for three days) and I was leery of him getting away again.

But it wasn't working. If he got even an inkling that I wanted him to walk in the direction of the barn, he'd just start dragging me backwards, and as hard as I would try to avoid getting into a pulling match with him, he was too quick, and I couldn't move quick enough to keep from putting pressure on the lead.

Choice

Once upon a time, I would've doubled down on the lead rope pressure. I'd have said, I won't drag you, but you are NOT allowed to drag me. I'd have used all my strength to stop him, and maybe even tried a harsher tool, like a rope halter to "make" him stop. (Spoiler alert: it wouldn't have worked. Pressure begets pressure.)

Instead, I did the only other alternative that I could see.

I took the halter off.

I probably could've just taken the lead rope off, but I knew he already had a very suspicious association with the halter, so I thought he'd have more confidence if it was gone entirely.

And he did.

Now that he had full control of his feet, he was much more willing to engage. He would come to me and touch the target (that I'd been trying to show him all along). He would get closer to the barn door every time. He would take a treat from me while I was inside the barn.

It took a bit of time, but he came into the barn of his own accord, touched the target, took his treat, and then scooted back outside. I couldn't have been happier!

He then followed me back to his pen, earned lots of treats, and when I tried again the next day – at liberty from the start – he walked right into the barn with confidence and started targeting all the obstacles that I had set up inside.

Today I don't need to put a halter on him to bring him in, but I can, and he'll lead like any of my other equines. He walks into the barn with confidence. The most likely issue we'll have is when I think we're done for the day, and he disagrees and doesn't want to leave to go back out with his friends.

I might've gotten to the point where I could lead him into the barn – then by association, every other new location in his lifetime – by using escalating force, but I would never have the relationship that I do with him today.

Bentley has taught me a lot about the value of choice, and it's a lesson I make use of often – if I'm ever struggling to teach a horse something new and find I'm getting in conflict with them or relying on lead rope pressure, I take the lead rope off. It gives the horse confidence to have control, and it makes me a much better trainer to take away that crutch.

Choice

How Horses See

A horse's eyes are placed on the side of his head, so he can see in almost any direction. He has two blind spots: one right under his nose, and one directly behind him.

This might seem like basic information, but it's important to keep in mind when you're working around your horse. Approaching a fearful horse at his shoulder is going to make him more comfortable, and, of course, you don't want to approach from directly behind a horse.

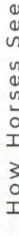
How Horses See

Horses also don't have depth perception or see colours in the way that we do, which can make a big difference in the way they see the world, and can significantly impact the way they respond. Moving their head up and down is an important part of how a horse judges depth. We've all seen them do it: they approach a novel stimulus (something new) and drop their head down to the ground and bob it up and down as they check it out. That movement of their head and neck isn't just expression, it's part of how they see.

While horses do see colours, they don't see the full spectrum that we do. Colours that are bright and obvious to us might blend in with the grass or dirt to them. With this information, when you're walking your horse up to, say, a plank that you want the horse to walk over. If the horse hesitates, it's very easy to respond by pulling on his halter and holding his head firmly to guide him towards the plank. However, if you're restraining his head, he literally can't see what you're asking him to walk on.

If that plank had a black stripe painted on it, for instance, it would be really hard for him to decide that it was a painted stripe ... or a hole he might fall in. This difference in how a horse sees depth and colour is so important to understand. When my horse who would jump anything ran right through a tiny 12" jump in an obstacle class, I'm pretty sure it wasn't because he just didn't feel like jumping, or thought he'd ruin my day by blowing a simple part of the course. I suspect the jump lined up poorly with the fence behind it, or the colour blended in, and if I'd noticed this possibility during the walkthrough and taken a different path to the jump, the outcome may have been different.

Another vision consideration is using blinders and check reins during driving. As a flight animal, horses rely on their exceptional range of vision to feel safe, and routinely using blinders is likely not the best choice for your horse, especially during early training when they're still figuring out the cart. Since horses need to be able to move their head and neck in order to have depth perception, restricting their head over uneven ground is a wildly bad idea, so unless you're driving on nothing but well-groomed arenas, ditch the overcheck.

How Horses See

REMEMBER: If your horse is struggling with an obstacle, shadow, or boogieman in the corner, remember that their eyes aren't seeing exactly what yours see, and that the freedom to move their head and neck is key to their ability to see.

My Experience

How Horses See

It was a dream of mine to drive my amazing horse Image on the beautiful trails at the Stonebridge Driving Club, but with his age and vision loss, a competition wouldn't have been appropriate. But a fall fun day was the perfect opportunity!

I was so excited to zoom around the trails behind the best horse I've ever driven.
But Image, who only had one eye, and reduced vision in the other, wasn't used to driving in the trees, and the shadows really threw him for a loop.

At first, he was so cautious, stopping often to reach down and touch the ground. Every time there was a distinct change in the appearance of the ground in front of him – a shadow, a damp area, a different soil – he would stop and investigate.

It was very interesting to watch him use his head and neck to improve his depth perception, and his whiskers and sensitive nose to explore the ground before he deemed it safe to step on.

While I'd long marveled at his ability to navigate his world using his whiskers, this day really showed me how much he relied on them, and was so impactful that I no longer trim whiskers on ANY of my horses. While I did trim whiskers for many years without noticing any detriment to my horses, being aware of how useful they are as a sensory organ meant that I could no longer, in good conscious, remove them.

I was perfectly happy to explore slowly with Image, chattering away to him from the cart as he checked out the footing and proceeded with great caution, but at one point another driving horse went by and he got very excited watching them go past. It was like he realized "oh, this place is for driving! It's safe!" and away he went, no longer concerned at all about the variation in footing, trusting my direction, and powering along at his biggest trot having a wonderful time.

It was a memory I'll always cherish – and also, a day that taught me a lot!

Breath Communication 10

Horses communicate a lot with their breath.

Holding their breath tells the rest of the herd they're concerned, or listening, aware of a potential threat. A loud snort says "get ready to run", and a deep slow breath means "all is well".

Horses don't know that we don't routinely use our breath to communicate, and we often don't even think about it.

Holding our breath is something we also do when we're nervous, but we are much more likely to be nervous about what the judge is going to think, than we are that something's going to eat us. Our horse doesn't know the difference though, to them, nervous is always "something might eat us" which means we need to become more aware of our own breathing, so we aren't inadvertently giving our horse bad information about our current situation.

One of the most valuable tools we can use to reassure our horse, when we see signs that they are approaching threshold, is to take a deep slow deliberate breath to show that we're not worried, and they don't need to be either.

Breath Communication

Because horses are so aware of breath, we are able to use it to further refine our communication with them. A breath prior to a cue or command helps let them know something is coming – a breath half-halt, so to speak. A deep slow breath can help them focus. They are so in tune to it, that I find I can get a downward transition in nearly any driving horse – even those who haven't learned the cue yet – simply with a deep relaxing breath. The cue of breath-"annnnd whoa" is one I believe every driving horse needs to understand very well, with the breath and the "and" allowing them to rebalance and prepare for the halt.

Using your breath to communicate with your horse can seem almost magical, as they are so in tune. I highly recommend experimenting with your horses. Go out and try holding your breath while standing near your horse and see their reaction. Next, try a big deep sigh and see how they respond to that. I think you'll be surprised how much your horse notices!

Breath Communication

REMEMBER: If you are not aware of your breathing, your horse definitely is. Using our breath to intentionally communicate with our horse is a valuable tool, and being careful to not inadvertently communicate something bad is important, too!

My Experience

Breath Communication

I first learned about breath communication during a seminar with Peggy Brown, a Centered Riding and Driving instructor. It made such an impact on me that I went home and immediately tried it out.

I was playing with Rocky, then a two year old stallion, seeing if he'd walk with me at liberty. Being a two year old stallion, he was easily distracted and would wander off, and when he did I'd give a big deep breath, and that was enough to regain his attention and bring him back to me, every single time. I couldn't believe it! I immediately started incorporating breath cues into everything I do with my horses, as well as just generally trying to be more aware of what my breath is doing when I'm with my horses.

The next time I really tested the concept was at a show. My mom had a headache, and asked me to drive her horse, Duke, in his classes. A notoriously sensitive guy, I hadn't driven Duke in a couple years, and I knew that he would already be taking offense at the change. He's also very fussy about rein cues, and in combination with a different driver, I was pretty sure that ANY sort of rein direction on a downward transition would've resulted in an open mouth, tension, and a less than pretty picture for the judge.

So even though he had no history of trained breath communication, when they called for the transition, I concentrated on not making any changes with my hands at all, and instead just breathing and using verbal cues: big breath "and walk" – and it worked!

This experiment in using breath communication resulted in no open mouthed drama from Duke, smooth and lovely transitions, and even a Reserve Championship!

Needless to say, I now use breath communication in everything I do with my horses, but as it's one of those things that take time to build into a habit, I know I could still do more and continue to make it a goal for myself.

Opposition Reflex 11

There are some horses that always respond to pressure with more pressure, to the point that you have to be careful with them as their reactions can become dangerous. However, every horse's natural response to pressure IS pressure.

It's called Opposition Reflex, and it's something that, in the wild, served horses very well. Picture a wild horse being attacked by wolves. The wolf reaches up and grabs the soft part of the horse's belly. If the horse pulled away from that bite, the teeth of the wolf would tear open his belly and likely result in the death of the horse. If instead he pushes into the pressure, not only does he minimize the damage from the bite, but he has a great chance of pushing the wolf off balance, trampling him and getting away.

Opposition Reflex

We see the effects of this instinct all the time when we're working with horses. From foals pulling back against their first halter and lead, to horses leaning on you when you try to get them to move away, or running into you when something spooks them.

The trouble is, in the moment, we're more likely to anthropomorphize and call them "stubborn" or "disrespectful," or who knows what sort of colourful names, which predisposes us to add more pressure, creating a cycle that is likely to end in an unfair situation for a horse who is simply behaving in the only way he knows how to.

Horses can absolutely learn to respond to cues that work against the ingrained Opposition Reflex. We do it all the time, teach them to respond to a pressure cue. But that process of learning will go much smoother if we are aware of the instinct we're working against, and rather than escalating the pressure, instead use as little pressure as possible, reward the smallest effort and build gradually as your horse begins to understand.

Understanding Opposition Reflex is even more important when we are dealing with Miniature Horses, as they are small and it is very tempting to just push them around and put them where we need them. If you've ever watched a youth halter obstacle class, with small children unsuccessfully attempting to shove their horse through a back or a sidepass, you've seen opposition reflex at work.

It's a big part of why you hear people claim all Miniature Horses are "stubborn" or "nasty" – because rather than having things explained to them, as people are obligated to do with a thousand pound horse, they're pushed around and manhandled.

I might be nasty, too, if that was the case!

Opposition Reflex

REMEMBER: When teaching your horse a new skill, it's important to reinforce the small efforts, so that they have time to understand what you're asking, rather than trying to force them to do the finished movement and come up against their opposition reflex.

My Experience

Opposition Reflex

When I was a little girl, my Grandad bought four black geldings that had previously been driven as part of an eight horse hitch. While they drove in their hitch okay, handling them on the ground was a different story

They would put their heads down and just pull, often getting away from an unsuspecting handler if they weren't prepared. And if you got between them, they would lean on you so hard their feet would skid out the other side. I have a vivid memory of brushing them and being squished between two of them, when I was barely able to see over their backs, and my Grandma grabbing me to rescue me.

Opposition Reflex

I know now that this behaviour was most likely caused by a lot of pressure in their previous training. They'd been pulled and pushed around, and so they'd learned to pull and push back.

They improved, gradually, as they learned that they weren't going to be shoved around as a default approach anymore, but they were always very "into pressure" horses. I remember Donner dragging one of my 4-Hers through the barn when he was 32.

Much more recently, we had (still have!) a horse named Tempest that was just increasingly dangerous about having his feet trimmed. He is a big strong horse (still Miniature, of course, but a tank!) and the more we tried to restrain him, the more his behaviour escalated, until we'd have four people trying to contain him and were legitimately afraid that someone – either horse or human – was going to get hurt.

When my Grandad and Grandma decided to retire from horse care, and their remaining 10 black geldings came here with the rest of the herd, Tempest was among them, and Grandad was so concerned about us getting hurt that I think he nearly didn't let us have him. He would ask me, even as his dementia worsened, about "that horse from Edmonton" and warn me to be careful around him.

But I'd spent some time with Tempest, and I figured out that he was a true "into pressure" horse, and the more we tried to restrain him, the harder he would fight.

After getting him comfortable with me handling his feet, I told my farrier what I'd learned – if he wants his foot back, you give it to him, right now, no questions asked.

Making that shift made all the difference. Today, knowing that he can have his foot back if he needs it, and that we're never going to push hard enough to get him on the fight, Tempest is trimmed without any extra help or any serious issues. No more rearing, kicking, or bodychecking, though he is a bit of a cookie monster – that's a trade off I'll take all day long!

It can be hard to make the choice to "let the horse win" but we have to remember, we're on the same team, and we're not supposed to be in conflict in the first place. We're far better off to avoid the opposition reflex in the first place.

Interpretation of Body Language

12

Watching the body language of our horse as they respond to a situation or training approach is a huge part of understanding their responses. Often, you'll hear someone say the horse "blew up out of nowhere!" but that is almost never true – the exception would be a horse in a state of learned helplessness, who has given up reacting at all, until they're pushed too far.

Being aware of what our horse is trying to tell us can help us earn our horse's trust and keep both ourselves and our horse safe. While signs of concern or discomfort will vary from horse to horse, they can be as subtle as turning their head away or holding their breath.

Spending time with your horse outside of training can be a great way to start to read their signals. Watching them with other horses is a fabulous tool – how do they react when they find themselves in a conflict with another horse, or when a sudden sound catches their attention? Everything you can learn by watching will help you in your interactions with them in the future.

Often, we humans misinterpret the body language of our horses as aggressive or dominating, when they're actually just trying to tell us that they need a little space or time. While, of course, there are some behaviours that we cannot allow, and need to respond to for our own safety, we need to immediately attempt to deconstruct what led up to the behaviour, so we know how to avoid the horse feeling like they need to respond in that manner in the future.

Body Language

Regardless, giving the horse the benefit of the doubt is always going improve your relationship with your horse. In most cases, behaviour such as turning their hindquarters towards you, or pinning their ears, is defensive, not aggressive, and punishing it is likely to make a fearful horse even more fearful.

Avoid punishment whenever possible, and instead of using labels like "disrespectful" or "aggressive" look at all body language as more information you can use to understand your horse's emotional state.

Our own body language is worth careful consideration as well. Horses are a prey animal, and humans are a predator. Often, without even thinking about it, our body language may be predatorial and a sensitive horse will become defensive. Things like direct eye contact, squared shoulders, sudden movements, and even outstretched hands with fingers spread out can be too intense for some horses. By simply lowering our focus, approaching at angle, moving slowly, and offering the back of a gently folded hand for them to sniff, we can reduce our inadvertently aggressive stance and make a timid horse more comfortable.

Interpretation of Body Language

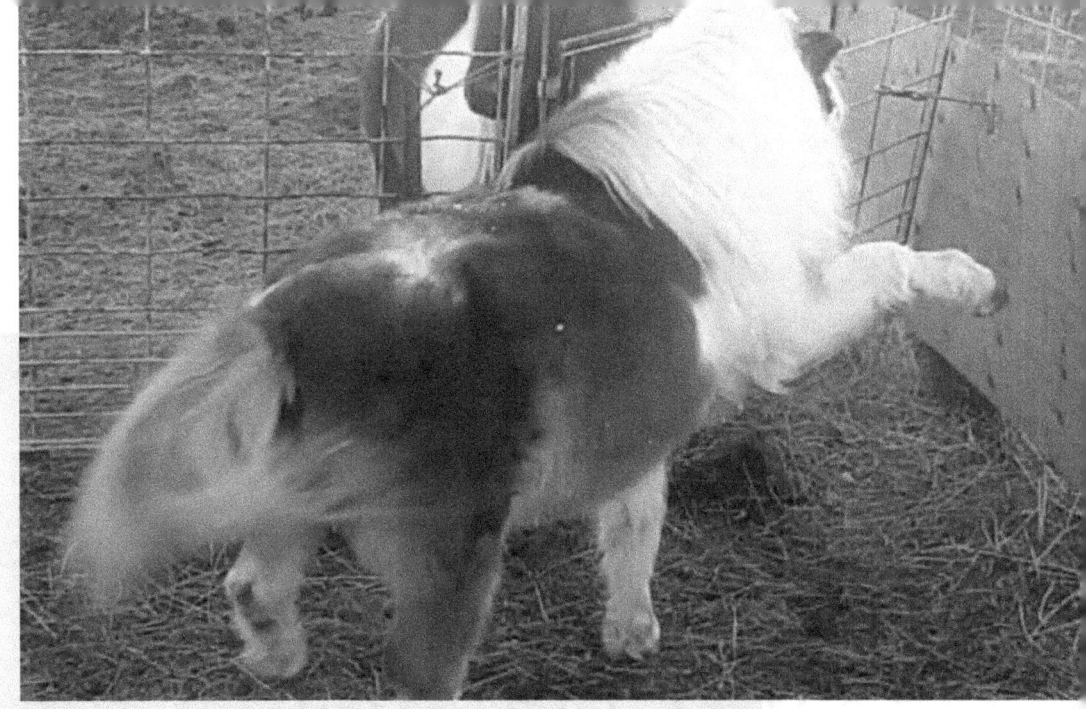

REMEMBER: Every horse is an individual and blanket interpretations of body language are unlikely to be accurate. Figuring out the cause of the behaviour is going to be far more effective than a knee-jerk reaction. Likewise, horses may misinterpret our body language and appearing less predatorial can make a big difference in how our horse responds.

My Experience

Interpretation of Body Language

My friend Julia and I have run workshops for kids together using our Miniature Horses, and it always amazes me how children, most of whom have no previous experience with horses at all, are much better able to read their body language than are "horse people".

Oly, who I talked about earlier in this book, was at his crankiest stall rest time when a little girl approached him. He pinned his ears and swung his head at her and she calmly stepped back. I asked her, "What did Oly say to you?" and she said, "He asked me to please leave him alone right now."

Body Language

If we, as horse people, could let go of our fear, and the years of being taught about "respect" and "teaching them who's boss", we would all have a much better relationship with our horses. But it isn't easy. Even knowing what I know, there are situations where I react first and think later. Luckily, horses are resilient and forgiving, and all we can ever do is be better next time.

I think if I could see pinned ears or a turned bum and instead of thinking, "cut that out!" my default was, "I wonder what he's trying to tell me? How could I make him more comfortable?" then I'd be pretty happy with how my horsemanship has evolved.

Body language goes beyond the big reactions and obvious attempts at communication. We can identify discomfort and pain by the wrinkles in their nose, the shape of their eye, the position of their ear. We subconsciously see more than we are able to consciously be aware of, too.

One evening I went out to do chores, brought Image into his stall, and instead of digging into his dinner of warm soaked cubes like normal, he laid down. Uh oh! Huge alarm bells.

He didn't seem colicky to me, though that would've been a major colic symptom. I watched him all evening, and something told me "he has a headache" – I chatted with my vet, gave him some banamine, and watched him all night.

In the middle of the night, after checking on him, I was flipping through the photos I'd taken of him earlier in the evening, and finally I saw it – his face was asymmetrical! The next time I went out to the barn, sure enough, he had a painful lump above his eye, and the swelling was affecting his facial nerve, making one side of his face droop very slightly.

A few days of anti-inflammatories and he was fine, back to normal, but I'm sure that my "he has a headache" instinct was because I was seeing that change in his face, as well as signs of pain in his expression, without being consciously aware of it.

Trust your intuition. Like those kids, we know more than we think, but we second guess ourselves.

Habituation 13

Introducing a horse to new things is definitely a good idea, but it's the way in which it is done that is important.

Habituation is the scientific term for what many people commonly would refer to as desensitizing. The official definition of habituation is a form of learning in which an organism decreases or ceases its responses to a stimulus after repeated or prolonged presentations. Essentially, the organism learns to stop responding to a stimulus which is no longer biologically relevant.

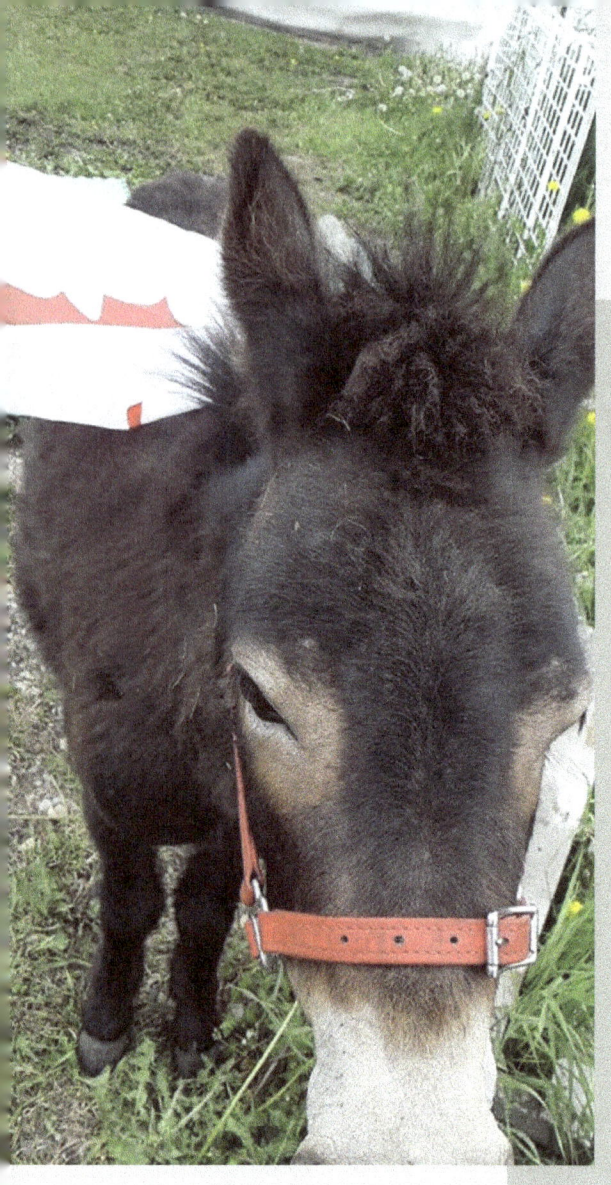

Habituation

Horses do this on their own all the time – for example, my barn is a tent building, and when the snow falls off the roof it makes quite a unique sound. Initially, horses make a huge jump when the snow falls, and are very alarmed. As it continues to happen, however, they learn that it isn't affecting them at all, and is simply an odd noise. Eventually, they react very little, or sometimes not at all – it often makes me jump more than it does the horses who spend a lot of time in the barn.

When we are introducing a horse to something new that we'd like them to become habituated to, we want to be sure that we don't inadvertently sensitize them to it and make them more frightened than they would have been on their own. That means really listening to them, and being aware of all the other concepts that we've talked about so far: we want to watch their body language, make sure we aren't pushing them over threshold, and use our own breath communication to show we aren't worried. We can use stroking and scratching to help activate the CARE system, or use target training or approach conditioning (allowing the horse to follow the new item) to help activate the SEEKING system.

We also need to be sure that we avoid using flooding when introducing our horses to something new. Flooding is the process of overwhelming a horse with a new stimulus, without possibility of escape, until they learn that nothing they do makes a difference so they simply shut down. The idea of "sacking out" a horse, touching them with a flag or plastic bag all over without stopping until they stop reacting is a form of flooding.

The horse doesn't learn that they don't need to be scared, instead they learn that it doesn't matter if they're scared, which is going to significantly undermine the trust and partnership with their human.

While there are many ways to approach helping our horses habituate, we want to avoid flooding and learned helplessness at all costs.

Habituation

Habituation

REMEMBER: When habituating a horse to a new item or situation, our goal isn't for them to stop reacting, but rather to no longer be afraid and become truly comfortable.

My Experience

Habituation

One of the biggest places where we, as Miniature Horse people, don't tend to spend enough time on habituation is driving training.

We're attaching a wheeled projectile to a flight animal. They need to be TRULY comfortable with it.

Unfortunately, this a situation when people often accidentally use flooding – the horse is so overwhelmed that they don't react, and the human is lulled into thinking all is well, when the horse does give a big reaction.

Habituation

Habituation to the cart needs to go as slow as the horse needs. My horse Rocky took four years (granted with some health issues and a major surgery for me in the middle of that slowing things down a bit!) before he was to the point where he felt confident just hooking up to the cart. And that's okay.

People would ask me why I wasn't driving him at the show, as they'd seen photos of him driving at home, and I would say, "he's just not ready." Because he wasn't.

Even once he was comfortable with the cart, at the walk, for a long time, trotting wasn't possible for him. He hadn't yet figured out how to balance the cart and driver at a faster speed, so he would just stop after a few steps of trot, until I helped him build the strength and balance to be confident.

Today he's my most reliable "hook up and go" horse, and I'm so glad I took as long as he needed.

I've worked with horses who've been started right from the beginning in blinders, never really knowing what was following them. After a scary incident they have had to go back to habituating to simply standing between the shafts for a long time before we were able to even think about hooking them up.

Habituation takes the time it takes, but having a horse that's truly comfortable with what you're asking them to do is worth every single second.

Learned Helplessness 14

Learned helplessness is defined as behavior that occurs when the subject endures repeatedly painful or otherwise aversive stimuli which it is unable to escape from or avoid. After such experiences, the organism often stops attempting to escape or avoid even painful and frightening situations, as they've learned that nothing they do makes any difference in their situation.

Unfortunately, learned helplessness is too common in horses. The horses who are "bombproof" and never react to anything, the ones that perform their job like a robot, accurate but not enthusiastic, often with a dull expression and unfocused eyes – we've all seen them, and once you learn to recognize them it's alarming how often you'll see them.

Learned Helplessness

Generally, learned helplessness is more likely in a training system that uses strong aversives as negative reinforcement and positive punishment, minimal positive reinforcement, and giving the horse no choice or control over their situation.

Trainers who say things like "he doesn't get to say no" "don't let him win" or "he's disrespectful" are red flags that their methods are in danger of creating a horse in a state of learned helplessness.

While a horse in a state of learned helplessness may seem to be "desirable" as they often appear docile and well behaved, they are also more likely to have a dramatic and dangerous reaction when something penetrates their ability to shut out the world. The horses who truly do "blow up out of nowhere" may have been flooded or in a state of learned helplessness prior to their reaction. While some forms of training use a state of learned helplessness to "break" a horse (usually inadvertently by a trainer who doesn't understand the implications), it's easier than you may think to "flood" a horse and set up this state of being unable to respond.

Unfortunately, due to their small size, I think it's easier for people who work with Miniature Horses to get carried away and accidentally do this.

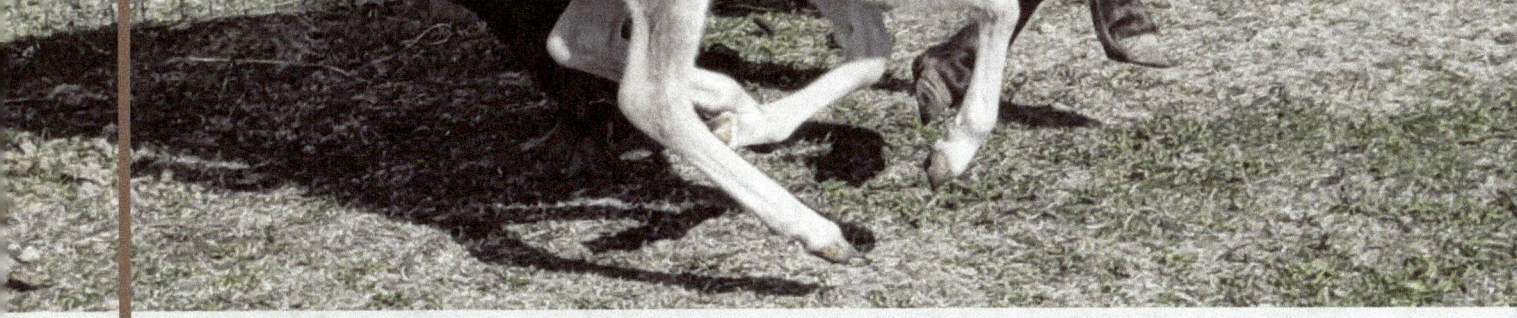

The most common example I see is driving training. People decide they are going to train a horse to drive. They start putting the harness on, and it goes well, so they start ground driving them and it goes well so they put the cart on, just to see, and the horse doesn't react, so they get in and away they go, and before they know it in one day they've thrown new equipment, new stimulus, new cues, and attached a wheeled projectile to their flight animal. It's gone "well," not because the horse understood any part of it, but because it was so far out of the horse's comfort zone that they're overwhelmed and not able to respond.

But they will respond one day, when they manage to "wake up" from their flooded state, and their FEAR response kicks in. I hear too often "I don't know what changed, they were so good when I first started driving them!"

If you have a horse that you think may be in a state of learned helplessness, allowing them time to "be a horse" with access to the Three F's, and introducing a new training system with choice, control, and positive reinforcement, will help them to recover. Be warned, however, that they are not going to be the same "well trained" horse when they do remember how to be a horse, so training should likely start over at the beginning. Once they understand that they DO have a choice and they CAN say no, you might see a lot of very big no's for a while, but it's worth it for when they actually choose to say yes.

Learned Helplessness

REMEMBER: By listening to your horse, using training that is Least Invasive and Minimally Aversive with good timing, monitoring their emotional state, and ensuring they have a voice in their training, with choice and control over how things progress, you'll be able to prevent a state of learned helplessness.

My Experience

Learned Helplessness

A friend of mine had a horse that they started in harness. They took their time and did the very best they could for their horse. They believed that the horse understood every step along the way.

At their first show, the horse ran away, a terrifying experience for both horse and driver, and one that the horse still hasn't mentally recovered from.

I believe that, despite the best efforts of my friends, their horse was in a state of learned helplessness. They were "going along," not because they understood, but because they were overwhelmed and didn't feel they could react.

When the additional stress of a show happened, it was enough to break through, and when the reaction finally happened, it was BIG.
Miniature Horses are very accommodating. They will "go along" often whether they truly understand or not. In driving training especially, going even slower than you think you should, moving on to the next stage only after having thoroughly tested their understanding of the previous stage, and watching so closely for body language and signs they are approaching threshold are so important.

It's easy to be fooled. Really listen to your horse, give them every chance to have a voice in what you're doing, and you'll be on the right track!

Scientific Method

According to Wikipedia, "The scientific method is an empirical method of acquiring knowledge that has characterized the development of science since at least the 17th century. It involves careful observation, applying rigorous skepticism about what is observed, given that cognitive assumptions can distort how one interprets the observation."

Scientists create a hypothesis based on their previous understanding, and then design an experiment to test that hypothesis. They use the data they gather as a result to inform their next experiment, and there's no such thing as a failure, as they're continually learning from the results.

As horse trainers, we use our previous experiences and knowledge to make a training plan, but unfortunately, we tend to allow our emotions to cloud our evaluation of the results. We think horses are "being bad" or "being stubborn" when they're just telling us that they don't yet understand what we're asking, or that something is bothering them.

If we approached our horsemanship more like a scientist, we could look at the information we gather from each attempt dispassionately and use it to inform – and improve – our next efforts. Instead of taking it personally or getting frustrated when things aren't going the way we thought they would, we can evaluate what's happening, and think critically about the variables involved, and see what happens if we make a change on our next effort. We can use this same method to evaluate our own skills.

Understanding when we are most likely to react poorly can help us minimize how often it happens.
Using video can help us see more clearly what was effective and where we could improve. It can help to remember that just like our horses, we're learning every day, and we need to give ourselves the time and space to improve, just as we do our horses.

Approaching training scientifically can allow both our horses and ourselves to continue to learn and improve.

Scientific Method

Scientific Method

Remember: Horses don't give wrong answers, it's all just information. You can use that information to formulate a better plan for your next attempt to help your horse learn. You're on the same team as your horse – don't let your emotions convince you otherwise.

My Experience

Scientific Method

I find keeping my emotions out of training a real challenge. Earlier this year, I was struggling with an agility course with Little Duke – he didn't want to trot, I needed him to trot, and we were both just getting frustrated with each other. The more frustrated I got, the worse a trainer I was, and the less he wanted to participate, and then I'd get so upset that I was ruining this thing that he used to enjoy. It became a vicious cycle, getting worse and worse.

Here's how I approached the problem.

First, I asked what wasn't working, and what I could change. In this specific case, that meant moving the course outdoors, despite the snow. There is no use continuing to do the same thing over and over – nothing is going to change unless you make a change.

Second, when I start to get frustrated, I make myself stop. It's so easy to just ask harder, or more, but that never works. If your horse doesn't understand the small cue, why would he better understand the bigger one? It's not easy, but I have to stop, and it helps if I say, out loud, "well, that's not working, is it? How can I help you understand what I want?" And if I can't find an adjustment to try at that moment, then it's best to walk away. No one wins if it turns into a fight. Try again tomorrow when you're both rested.

Third, remember that it's just information. No matter how badly it's going, you're gathering data. I learned that Little Duke doesn't want to trot inside the barn. That's good information, and doesn't need to be frustrating at all – how can information be frustrating?

Fourth, keep it short. The longer I work with a horse, the worse I am at training and they are at learning. I've implemented a 10 Minute Rule, and if I'm super focused on a new agility course or new trick or any other skill, then I'll actually set a timer to remind me. It doesn't matter if it's going well and I'd like to try one more time, or if it's going badly and I'd like to try one more time. One more time is almost never a good idea.

You might come up with your own rules and coping skills, but however you can keep your emotions out of it, see every attempt as information, and remember that you and your horse are on the same team, you're doing great!

Thank You!

I hope the information in this book helps you to have a more productive and enjoyable relationship with your Miniature Horse!

Because you choose to read this book, I already know that your horses are lucky to have a human like you, that continues to question and learn to improve their skill.

Have fun with your horses, and I hope that I will see you in the Miniature Horsemanship Community, either online or in real life!

Kendra

www.ingramcontent.com/pod-product-compliance
Lightning Source LLC
Chambersburg PA
CBHW081122080526
44587CB00021B/3706